Provoking Thoughts

By Gina Blaze
Foreword by David Wagner
Illustrated by Lisa Leach

Dedication

"It takes all kinds" . . . in the journey of life we meet all kinds of people. Those people are in our path to teach us something. Some make us laugh, some help us to see, some give us courage and hope, some challenge us, and some make us cry.

This dedication is for my friend. Her life has been filled with great challenges, successes and failures - but through it all she chooses to love above everything. She floats.

I've watched her, and I have thought to myself, she must ask this question everyday . . . "How can I love more?" God answers and uses her as a beautiful waterfall of His continuous love over everyone she encounters on the journey of life. I came under that waterfall. Our paths crossed many years ago, and in that moment we connected for life. I am so thankful for that.

To you my friend: I can celebrate this book because of you. The cheerleader inside of you kept me writing. The encourager in you made me persevere. The friend in you loved me in the times that were dark and hard. The giver in you gave to me with no expectations and with complete joy. The laughter in you gave me medicine for my soul. Most of all, the "Pray-er" in you exemplified a life in prayer to God that caused my life to change for the better.
You have taught me more about love through your pure heart and devotion to Jesus. I love you and it makes my heart happy to write these words of dedication to you.

I, Gina Blaze, dedicate this book "Provoking Thoughts" to my sister and friend, Madeline Balletta.

Acknowledgements

Twenty years ago a man named Denny Cramer prayed over me and said, "There is a gift in your hands." I never dreamt that the gift would be this book. *Thank you Denny, for prophesying this book into existence.*

David Wagner and Judy Shaw are my heroes of faith. There is an old saying, "The teacher appears when the student is ready." I've watched you both lay your lives down over and over, living out what's on these pages. In the last 12 years of doing life together you have seen me at my best and also at my worst - and still, you love me. True love has no greater meaning than laying your life down for your friend.
Thank you both. You are true blue.

Maggie Johnson, Donna Somma, Patti Canfarotta, Susan Reens, Michele Caporizzo, Nancy Henkes, and Jackie Bausch - I am so thankful for each of you. I would have giant holes in my heart without you. Your constant source of encouragement and prayers has kept my tank full. *I love you.*

Barbara Gradia - You were my battery charger, Thanks for getting me started on the road to publishing!

Lauren Corso and Vera Barroso – My interns, who turned into spiritual daughters. Whenever I needed you, you came running! *Thank you!*

Sam Maskell and Mary Algiere – The problem solvers. My stealth help behind the scenes, always making sure everything's all right! God sees your kindness and giving hearts. *Thank you!*

Erin Kulak and Lisa Leach - One, a master of excellence and the other a creative genius. This book would not have become whole without the two of you. Wherever God decides to take it, remember you are both on every page. *My deepest gratitude to both of you, Thank you.*

A page of their own . . .

Pat Lanza, I want to acknowledge you for your example of the most giving person I have ever known. I learn something every time I am in your presence. *I hope you enjoy this book.*

Someone asked me "Do you know how blessed you are?"
My answer is, "Yes I do."
The more I come to know and understand the Word of God regarding family, honor, blessing and love - the more I know how truly blessed I am. The three people who mean everything to me live true to themselves and true to God. Dan, Lindsay and DB, you three rock my world. We are family. There has never been a dull moment! We have loved, believed, laughed and cried together, stood up for one another, and bared each other's burdens. We've had our fights and found our way out. But most of all, I can say it loud and proud, we pray for one another. I know how much you pray for me. It's only by God's grace and faith that has moved mountains that this life of love, laughter and loyalty has surrounded us. You are all a dream come true. *I love you. I am so thankful for you. I am blessed. Forever a Blaze!*

Most importantly, I thank you, God.
Your book inspired me to write this book.
This is my personal "Provoking Thought" from you:

"Finally, whatever is true, whatever is honorable, whatever is just, whatever is pure, whatever is lovely, whatever is commendable, if there is any excellence, if there is anything worthy of praise, think about these things."

My prayer, is that You Jesus ~ will be honored by this book.

Foreword

You are about to read an amazing book filled with truth, revelation, knowledge, and wisdom that the Holy Spirit has graciously deposited into my sister in the Lord, Gina Blaze. Gina is one of the most faith-filled and faithful people I have ever known. She is a constant source of encouragement, wisdom, kindness, love and prayer. Gina is full of the word, life, joy, and the Holy Spirit all of which are released on the pages of this book.

Gina's passion and love for God and His people is second to none. I have had the great honor of calling Gina Blaze a sister, friend, co-laborer, and encourager. Over the past 12 years, I have watched as Gina and her husband Dan have served and prayed tirelessly for the Church in New England and around the globe. Gina continually helps people realize their God given purpose and to accomplish their dreams. Provoking Thoughts is another tool that God has given Gina to inspire His people.

Hebrews 10:24 says: "Let us consider how to stir up and provoke one another to love and good works." I can honestly say that Gina is a person who constantly stirs me up and provokes me to love and good works. She continually encourages and pushes myself and others to grow closer to Jesus and to dream big.

This book is filled with spiritual truths, precious gems, golden nuggets, and heavenly encouragement. Each page is filled with truth and love that God has whispered to Gina over the years. I can honestly say that Gina has not only written and shared these provoking thoughts, but she carefully lives them out on a daily basis.

I believe that this book will encourage you and bring you into a deeper personal encounter with the love and knowledge of God.

Blessings and Miracles,

David Wagner

Contents

Contents

Introduction

If this book has found its way into your hands, it is my hope that you will ponder the simple truths in it. Honestly, most of what is written are not my own truths, but given to me through the words of Scripture. God has deliberately chosen to use ideas the world considers foolish and of little worth in order to get to the heart of those people considered by the world as wise and great.

Life's journey has allowed me to sit with many people and listen to stories of shattered hopes and dreams. People struggling with deep-rooted hurts, feeling like life has crashed around them, not knowing which way to turn. They have gotten way off track in their thinking. I believe there is a way out, a way back, and a way through to the right path.

As a man thinks in his heart, so he is. Our minds can be a breeding ground for confusion or a think tank tendered with clarity and wisdom. It's our thoughts that rule over our lives and only one thought can be changed at a time.

Provoking Thoughts was created to accomplish just that – To provoke thoughts! If you find yourself pondering a statement from a page in this book it will have accomplished what it was meant to do. To do its job, let this book read you. Let the words and the artwork speak to your heart. I believe it will be an agent of change in your life.

I welcome you with open pages to contemplate and agree with Truth. One nod of the head, one yes, one whisper, "that's true," changes everything.

> "Watch your thoughts, for they become words.
> Watch your words, for they become actions.
> Watch your actions, for they become habits.
> Watch your habits, for they become character.
> Watch your character, for it becomes your destiny."
>
> ~ Unknown Author

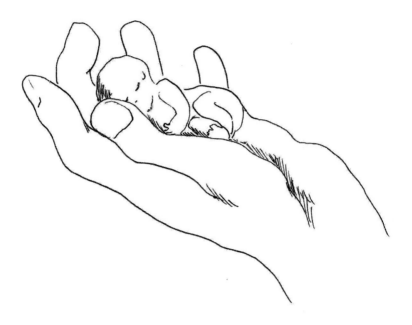

Life

With a breath and a heartbeat life begins,
and with a breath and a heartbeat it ends.
Life is fragile, precious, and a gift.

*"There are only two ways to live your life.
One is as though nothing is a miracle.
The other is as though everything is a miracle."*
                                        ~ Albert Einstein

Surviving or thriving? How are you living?
Life has essentials - nothing money can buy: water, sleep, breath,
nutrition, physical activity, giving and receiving love, forgiveness,
acceptance, thankfulness, and prayer.

In the moment is the only place where life really is.
Stay in the moment! . . . NOW!
Don't let something or someone steal your today . . .
Live Life Now! *Today is the only day you have.*
The preserver is this.
"He who guards his mouth, preserves his life."

Frank Sinatra sang this famous song: **"That's Life"** . . .
"I've been a puppet, a pauper, a pirate, a poet, a pawn and a king. I've
been up and down and over and out and I know one thing,
each time I find myself flat on my face, I pick myself up and get back in
the race."
***Pick yourself back up today; nobody is going to do it for
you.***

Life has an urgency to it. Do you need Life-Support?
CPR - Christ's Promised Response - ***He is the Life-Savior***.

Psalm 23 is not a funeral psalm. Do you know that goodness
and mercy are following you every day of your life?

*" . . . I have set before you life and death . . . **Choose Life.**"*

Order

If you have ever watched a courtroom scene, or if you have ever been to court yourself, you would hear –
"Order in the Court." Everyone would rise for the judge
and there would be silence, respect and honor.

God has an Order – and **"It is good."**
Everything in life has an order: marriage, family, job, communication, creation - everything!

There is a beginning to everything and there is an end -
except for what's eternal. God is the Author and the Finisher
of your life and mine; the chapters are still being written.

In the order of creation God gave us keys for today:
He said, **"Let there be light." "It is good."**
"I made you in My image." "Rest."

What if, in every situation and circumstance in your life,
you began to say, ***"Let there be light."***

What if, first thing in the morning, you spoke these words to yourself:
"It's going to be a Good Morning."

When you look into the mirror, do you smile back at the face you see?
Do you realize whose **"image"** you have?

What if you shut down everything today and just took a **rest**?
Too simple? . . . Consider the possibilities.

Order your day:
"To stand every morning and thank and praise your God."

❖   *1 Chronicles 23:30*

Time

"It's about time" - that's when we are really listening.

Do you know what time it is?
Time is a teacher and a healer. It has wings of some sort
because it flies, so why does it take so long to get there?
Sports teams and children get time-outs; they call it strategy time.
Some people are before their time or ahead of it -
pioneers and thinkers.

There really is no time like the present, because it is a present.
We sometimes forget who gave it to us.

Vows of good times and bad times are often changed over time.
A friend loves at all times . . . who's your friend?
That settles that.

Can we really kill time, or save time in a bottle?
When it comes to time there is either plenty of it, or never enough. Use
your time. There is no waste of time in lessons learned.

In life there can be moments when we feel like we are out of time.
Don't wait. *"Say it in the living years."*

There is a moment in God that is an atomic second
and it changes life forever. You're here, still breathing . . .
Your purpose and mine are not finished yet - ***only time will tell.***
Stop . . . Pray . . . and Listen. It's not over until He says.

What matters? You can't be in two places at once,
so wherever you are, be fully there. **Live life now, real time.**

Now that's Big Time!

Season

To everything *there is* a season;
(the secret is in the season).
If you find out what season you're in,
you can live more fully within the boundaries of that season.

"A time for every purpose under heaven:

A time to be born and a time to die;

A time to plant, and a time to pluck what is planted;

A time to kill and a time to heal;

A time to break down and a time to build up;

A time to weep and a time to laugh;

A time to mourn and a time to dance;

A time to cast away stones, and a time to gather stones;

A time to embrace and a time to refrain from embracing;

A time to gain and a time to lose;

A time to keep and a time to throw away;

A time to tear and a time to sew;

A time to keep silence and a time to speak;

A time to love and a time to hate;

A time of war and a time of peace."

❖ *Ecclesiastes 3*

God makes everything beautiful in its time.
Just wait a minute.

ETERNITY is never-ending time with God.

New Beginnings

Is a new beginning really possible for you or me?
We don't have to wait for the opportunistic moment –
to be chosen for reality TV or to win the lottery.
A brand new start - How will that happen? Where do we start?
START SOMEWHERE!

Work it. Humble beginnings reap a prosperous future.
Ask the former generation. They did it with nothing!
You and I have five good senses.
Put your antennas up and use them. Take the step.
Just do it. Put your hand on the plow and don't look back.
"Don't despise the day of small beginnings."

What if I begin to sink?
The harder you struggle the more you sink. There is a way
through the wilderness and there are streams in the desert.

New mercies are waiting every morning. There is an open doorway at
the beginning of your day. Go through it with prayer.
That prayer is the light in your tunnel.
Keep moving. Sing that new song. Spring up on those feet.
Throw that old cane away.

Faith is often spelled R-I-S-K.
If you really want a new beginning, everything connected
with that old way of life has to go. A new beginning needs a new heart
– one that beats in agreement with God for His promises.

A New Beginning . . . you get a brand new one every day.
The promise with it is connected with your destiny.

> ❖ *Find out what Jeremiah 29:11 says.*
> ❖ *Begin there.*

Faith -
Believing God.

"If you don't believe - it's ok, just believe that I believe."
~ Joe Sekelsky

Faith is the difference between impossible and possible.

There is not a person on earth who is not believing for something. If we measure our faith through Scripture, there are two kinds: one is dead and one is alive.

Faith that is dying is dying because of fear.
Without a course of action, faith is dead.
Dead faith lives in a land of excuses without pursuit of God.
Dead faith gave up its legal right to hope.
Dead faith doesn't please God.

Alive faith requires something from us: *Listening.*
Alive faith obeys, believes, sees, speaks, prepares and receives.
Alive faith asks, seeks and knocks.
Alive faith stretches past our own ability and strength into God's.
Alive faith celebrates life every day.

A life lived through faith holds the "Title Deed" of things hoped for.

"Now faith is the substance of things hoped for, the evidence of things not seen."
❖ *Hebrews 11: 1*

25

Hope

We all know that Hope doesn't really float.
It's quite the opposite . . .

Hope is a heavy anchor to our faith, stabilizing us so that
we don't float away.

You and I desperately need to **get a hold of hope.**
Maybe the problem is that we have a tendency in us to believe in an
illusion of hope . . .
"I hope I win," "I wish I could", etc.
Hope believes, it doesn't plead.

Let's face it: bad things happen. If you give up hope,
you commit spiritual suicide (living apart from God).
You may say, "I don't believe in God."
The Good News is - He believes in you.

If you let the God of all hope purify your heart with the One and Only
truc hope in life, you will overflow with an attitude of strength and
courage that trusts beyond a shadow of a doubt that . . .

"No matter what happens, it is going to be alright."
                              ~ Ralph DiNardo Sr.

Leave the outcome to God.

Grow Hope.

*"We also have joy with our troubles because we know that these
troubles produce patience and patience produces character, and
character produces hope. And hope will never disappoint us."*

                              ❖   *Romans 5:3-5*

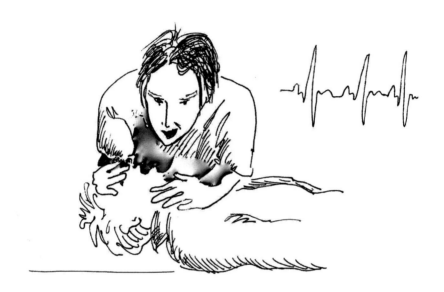

Love

Love . . . knows Me.
Heart, soul, mind, and strength.
Intimacy . . . in-to-me-see . . . God.

Love . . . one another.
Greater love lays down its life for his friend.
Love . . . happened over 2,000 years ago.
God so loved. God gave. Divine purpose. Eternal Life.

God is Love. He has a Kingdom and Royalty deserves loyalty.
In finding love, you will find righteousness, peace, and joy.
Close the door, pray, and you will find Love.

Love is heaven's force.
The force that compels us to move out of our comfort zone
and move into the supernatural zone.
The lost get found and what was dead comes to life.

Love your enemies - Divine Purpose.
Mercy – Divine Purpose.
Helping people find God – Divine Purpose.
Forgiving – Divine Purpose.
Giving - Divine Purpose.
Saying, "I love you" and meaning it – Divine Purpose.
Jesus - Divine Purpose.

He who has been forgiven much - *loves much.*

"Love suffers long and is kind; love does not envy; love does not parade itself, is not puffed up; does not behave rudely, does not seek its own, is not provoked, thinks no evil; does not rejoice in iniquity, but rejoices in the truth; bears all things, believes all things, hopes all things, endures all things. Love never fails."

❖ *1 Corinthians 13: 4-8*

29

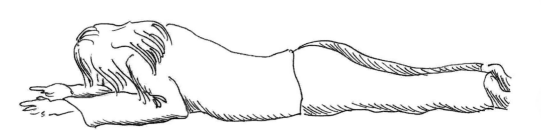

Prayer

- ❖ **Pray** for those who mistreat you.

- ❖ Always **pray** and don't give up.

- ❖ **Pray** that you will not fall into temptation.

- ❖ **Pray** in the Spirit on all occasions
  with all kinds of **prayers** and requests.

- ❖ Do not be anxious about anything, but in every situation,
  by **prayer** and petition, with thanksgiving,
  present your requests to God.

- ❖ Devote yourselves to **prayer**, being watchful and thankful.

- ❖ The **prayer** offered in faith will make the sick person well.

- ❖ The **prayer** of a righteous person is powerful and effective.

- ❖   . . . the **prayers** of God's people, went up before God from the
  angel's hand.

- ❖ Say thank you for answered **prayer.**

- ❖ Be faithful in **prayer** and watch your faith fill to overflowing.

*"God can work wonders through people who **pray.**
People can work wonders if they let God lead them in **prayer.**"*

*"Our Father in heaven, hallowed be Your name. Your kingdom come.
Your will be done on earth as it is in heaven. Give us this day our
daily bread. And forgive us our debts, as we forgive our debtors. And
do not lead us into temptation, but deliver us from the evil one. For
Yours is the kingdom and the power and the glory forever. Amen."*

- ❖ *Matthew 6:9-13*

Change

Change happens in a heartbeat, in the twinkling of an eye,
in a split second; everything can look and be different.

We've all heard these sayings:
"Change is in the air."
"Change is on the horizon."
"Change is coming."
"Change is here to stay."

The truth is: *life is full of changes* and for some, those changes
aren't easy. The key is to appreciate what you have today.
You may wake up tomorrow and find things very different.
Ready or not, change is inevitable.

Can you embrace change?
Difficult, yes.
Possible, yes.
Beneficial, yes.

Do you want personal change?
Are you willing to do what it takes? It takes work.
"When it becomes more difficult to suffer than change -
that's when real change happens."
The stinking thinking is what keeps you unchangeable -
Your mind dwelling on the past dead-ends you.
Turnaround, release control, get out of the driver's seat,
and give the steering wheel over to God.

Doing something different gets different results.

Revelation is the agent of change . . .

"I was blind, now I see."

That's change!

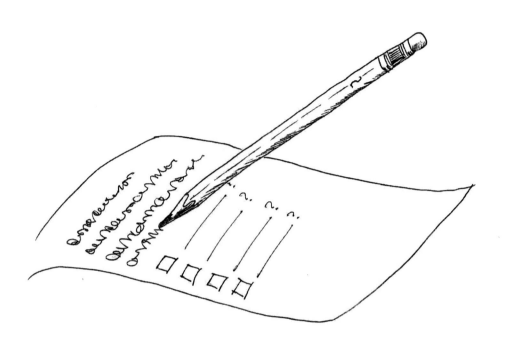

The Faith Test

Testing: one, two, three.
Testing Patience – **The ability to endure under pressure.**

The more difficult the circumstance, the stronger you become and patience matures. You won't have to take that same test again.

When you are feeling frustrated, use the **HALT** check:
Are you *Hungry, Angry, Lonely, Tired?*

Frustration leads to exaggeration!

That's worth repeating:

Frustration leads to exaggeration!

Today, every one of us is going to need to take that deep breath to get back on track when we derail.
If you lose your patience – **Find it fast!** Wait a minute, breathe, walk away, pray, repent, listen, laugh at yourself, and forgive.

WHEN YOU DON'T KNOW WHAT TO DO . . . WAIT!

Great news: **God is full of patience toward us.**
He wants our hearts to be established with an **unwavering faith**;
Position yourself to be still and watch His faithfulness.

"Count it all joy when you fall into various trials, knowing that the testing of your faith produces patience. But let patience have its perfect work, that you may be perfect and complete, lacking nothing. If any of you lacks wisdom, let him ask of God, who gives to all liberally and without reproach, and it will be given to him."

❖   *James 1: 2-5*

35

Strategy

We are all going through something, aren't we?
And the truth is, we really don't know
what's going to happen five minutes from now.
In our hearts we have plans, but it's God who determines our steps.

You may question, "What is His Will?"
His Will is His Word. It's worth reading!

Strategy: The book of Proverbs - A Think Tank.
"There is wisdom in many counselors."
"The tongue of the wise promotes health."
"He who walks with integrity walks securely."
"Love covers a multitude of sins".
"A righteous man regards the life of his animal."
"Counselors of peace have joy" – (who is your counselor?)
"The prudent are crowned with knowledge."
"A gentle answer turns away wrath."
"A gossip separates the best of friends."

Strategy holds a choice and a decision – a choice to stay fully in the
moments of today and to experience and enjoy what it holds.
Instead of trying to live in two places at once, decide to talk to God as
much as possible throughout the day . . . consistently.
Imagine the outcome of a life lived in conversation with God.

Here is a strategy:

*"Be joyful, pray continually and give thanks in all circumstances for
this is God's will for you in Christ."*

❖   *1 Thessalonians 5:16-18*

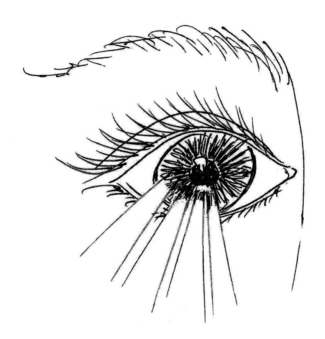

Focus

A point toward which light rays are made to converge.
Light attracts light spiritually, and like spirits attract naturally.

> *"Listen well to His words; tune your ears to His voice. Keep His message in your eyes at all times. Concentrate. Learn it by heart. Those who discover these words live – really live; body and soul, they're bursting with health."*
> ❖ *Proverbs 4:20*

Focus: Calls for attention, concentration, and understanding.
It's not plagued by panic or paranoia, but realizes a new day.
Every step you take with focus holds another key to walk straight,
straight into your promised land.

Focus: Our focus is on what we value most.

> *"No one can serve two masters. For you will hate one and love the other; you will be devoted to one and despise the other. You cannot serve both God and money."*
> ❖ *Luke 16: 13*

Focus: Begins with light in the eyes.

> *"You draw light into your body through your eyes, and light shines out to the world through your eyes. So if your eye is well and shows you what is true, then your whole body will be filled with light."*
> ❖ *Matthew 6:22*

God's Focus: He is watching with determination and radiance shining His light-force on you and me, the focus of His delight, with blessing and love.

> *"For the eyes of the Lord run to and fro throughout the whole earth, to show Himself, strong on behalf of those whose heart is loyal to Him."*
> ❖ *2 Chronicles 16:9*

Decisions, Decisions, Decisions

From the moment our eyes open until the end of our day,
you and I have made thousands of decisions.
Should I get up? Should I sleep 5 more minutes? What should I wear?
What should I eat? Should I go or should I stay?
Should I do this or do that?
We have all been given the freedom to choose.
We own every choice.

Life Choices: Decisions that will affect everything, with an
attachment of consequence or an attachment of promise . . .
Our choice.

Forewarned is Forearmed:
The warnings about traps laid in our path of decisions are in black and
white: Bible truth. Keep reading.

Traps: are built on schemes, lies and fears to destroy our destiny. Traps
complicate, confuse, steal, kill, and destroy.
They cause us to be selective with our hearing, relationships, emails,
texts and call-backs.
Temptations are traps if we give into them:
lust of the flesh, lust of the eyes, and pride.
Worry is a trap. Loving money is a trap.
Now for the BIG trap: Turning a deaf ear to wise instruction.

Choose Wisely: Don't be tossed in the waves.
No gray areas. Say yes or say no. Say what's true.
"I don't know" is not a decision.

*"Trust in the Lord with all your heart and lean not on your own
understanding in all your ways acknowledge Him and He will direct
your paths."*

                                     ❖   *Proverbs 3:5*

Responsibility

Responsibility has a face . . . and it's yours and mine.
We live in a "*name it and blame it*" world.
Nobody can ever be wrong! "It wasn't me!"
We shift blame, looking for someone to take the shame and the pain -
usually the person closest to us.

If you mess up, fess up! Don't give up!
The door to maturity has **responsibility** written on it.
Push on that door. Just do it - not with a blind eye or a deaf ear.

Your response is mixed with your ability.
Use your abilities. Respond with respect.

Responsibility will take you where you want to go.
Keep your word no matter what . . . Go there!
How do you know you are there? Lessons learned
and things working together for good.

Responsibility will keep you on the right track and profit you
more than you could imagine. Responsibility lets others see
that God is with you, commanding attention.

God keeps His word. He is responsible for it.
His message deserves a response -
one that's not common or ordinary: ***Love Him back.***

Be responsible. Ask for wisdom.

Wisdom is skill in living.

❖   ***Read Proverbs 4***

Understanding

Understanding: To know God and to be in awe of His words.

His ways are different than ours and His thoughts are higher than ours. We think we understand . . . Don't we?

Wisdom and understanding are partners. When understanding rests on a man or woman, that person has patience and kindness. They are problem solvers and use discretion. Wisdom, counsel, knowledge, strength, and peace flow from them like a river.
They would rather speak five words with understanding
than ten thousand that don't make sense.
That person wears grace like a beautiful necklace.

Wise counsel in a man's heart can be drawn from a well of deep insight. ***Words have power.*** We have been given a book filled with them. The Bible reveals in Proverbs 2 the value of wisdom and understanding. It's worth looking up.

Long life brings understanding because it's been tested over time. The richest man who ever lived on this earth was told he could ask for anything. He asked for an understanding heart to discern good and evil and God granted him that and so much more.

"It is possible to have understanding in order to know the mystery of God, whose name is Jesus, in whom are hidden all the treasures of wisdom and knowledge."

❖ *Colossians 2:2-3*

"Shallow understanding from people of good will is more frustrating than absolute misunderstanding from people of ill will."

~ Martin Luther King, Jr.

People

A young man wrote a letter to us. In it was this profound statement: **"People can be judgmental, manipulative, and real, all at the same time."** That is possible.

People are often misunderstood. Everybody deserves to be heard. Give a gift to someone - **Listen, Really Listen,** with patient understanding. Look them in the eyes and don't judge them.

Hold the phone! If you're on the other end and you want to be understood, **communicate**. If it's hard, **try harder,** and express yourself to others without hardness.

Are you judging somebody that you love?
Then you're watching too much "Idol."
Eat, Pray, Love is out of order.
It should be Love, Pray, and then Eat.
Television and movie fantasies will skew the emotions,
changing the way we deal with people.

Who are your people? Your people and my people are the ones that we love no matter what. **Cherish them.**
What about the unlovables? Can you cherish them, too?
What about the perfect ones, the hypocrites, and the bullies?
Perfection . . . is the enemy to excellence.
Hypocrisy . . . always wants to be seen by others.
Bullies . . . are wounded hearts and they need love.
To discern people is a gift; open it up and use it. It's built-in.

"All of life we are figuring out people." ~ Claire Thornson

So what matters? **Relationships.** What's important? **Love.**
Who are the people you need to reach today?

Life Lessons with people . . . that's where God comes in.

Labels

Are you a marked person?
How did those marks get on you anyway?
You and I may have an identity crisis
because of the pressure of a label.

She's this. He's that. They say. I heard. I know so and so.
I did this. I'm part of . . . I go to . . . He's worth . . .
She's such a . . . He's really . . . I have . . . I only buy . . .

Human nature labels. Bad as it is, we all do it and have it done
to us. Life is full of people marking people, making foolish
judgment calls that are based on wrong perceptions, leaving
irreversible tattoos.
We leave wrecking balls on reputations. **X** marks the spot . . .
right between the eyes on the target of our minds.

At times we wear somebody else's label.
We become "The Knock- Off." We think it will speak to others about
who we are because we fear what other people might say or think about
us. We are slaves to labels - riding a see-saw without a made-up mind.
One day up, one day down . . . wishy-washy.
Wishing we could wash those labels off.

God has a label and it's written on His thigh:
King of Kings and Lord of Lords - Revelation 19:16
Your real label is ***"Chosen by God,"***
and it's written on His heart. ***Finally Free!***

*"For the LORD does not see as man sees; for man looks at the outward
appearance, but the LORD looks at the heart."*

❖   *1 Samuel 16: 7*

Identity

Do you know what your name means? Find out!

"I knew your name before you were born. "
"I call you by name." ~ God

There is really more to you and me than meets the eye.
We have an identity. What really defines us?
We find out under pressure.

What's in your stuffing?
Hopefully it's made up of **Thanks and Giving.**

On the earth today are nameless, faceless, unique people of all colors
who do unbelievable acts of love, motivated by an unselfish nature.

Their identities are marked by God.
They say, "Greater is He who is in me."
They know, that what matters most, is:
What He says,
What He sees,
and that He is . . . the Center of Life.

Identity: solid as a rock.

The heart of the matter is Truth.
Read the Bible and let it read you.
Identity revealed.

Step up

Climbing a ladder in life? Where does it lead? Success? Power? Money? Stress? The next level may be hard to resist. Opportunities and temptations are waiting on every step.
Still climbing? Up is good as long as you're not afraid of heights.

How many rungs are on your ladder?
That rung may have a name attached to it –
It's that person who supported you on the way up so that you could go higher. The problem is, once you're up, you tend to forget them. Remember how that divine appointment happened - how that door opened for you, the one that was once closed tight?
Never forget the rung on your ladder.

There are steps to faith.
Those steps have **belief** and **hope** written on them.
Follow His footsteps . . . remember there's only one set in the sand.
The stepping stone of faith is not spiritual hopscotch.
It's a Rock that we stand on for security.

When everything is going right, it's like our steps are bathed in butter and cream. When all hell breaks loose, hold on for dear life - the ladder shakes.
On the ladder there are angels going up and down whispering, "Don't be afraid." Reach up while you're climbing. Take the grip of God's hand. He was there all the time.
Believe it or not . . .
He delights in every detail and orders every step.

*"A man's heart plans his way but the Lord
directs his steps"*

❖ *Proverbs 16:9*

53

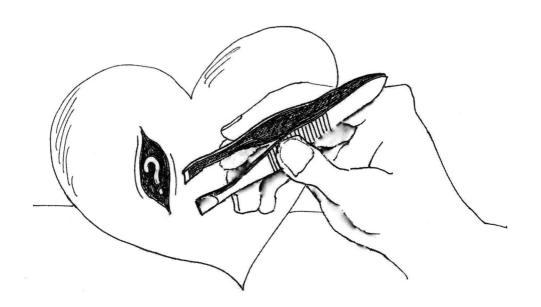

Motives

Who is watching anyway? Somebody is always watching!
Do you want your 15 minutes of fame or do you want God's applause?

Heart-checks can be a life-saver.

Motives cause us to act a certain way.
Motives have hidden agendas.
Motives can manipulate.

What was I thinking? It's not a trick question.
Why am I really doing this? Examine the motive.
How did I get myself into this? Quicksand.

Bad motives pollute pure hearts. They pull us away from the truth.
Impurities always need cleansing. There are seven spiritual purifiers:
Blood, Water, Fire, Fasting, Hope, Faith, and Truth.
We get a chance for internal cleansing if we are ***Honest to God.***

Heart checks can be a life saver.

We live in a fast talking, double-dealing, nobody-fights-fair world.
People are waiting to take the speck out of our eye
when the log is in their own.
Some are motivated by the need to control. One hand has a finger
pointed and the other hand is pushing buttons.
You and I don't have to fight our battles the same way.
Slow down . . . God Speaks.
Words are the voice of the heart.

Heart-checks can be a life-saver.

*"Create in me a clean heart, O God, and renew a steadfast spirit
within me."*
> ❖　*Psalm 51:10*

The Great Wall of Offense

Offenses will come. Sparks will fly.
Offenses weigh a lot. Why carry them?
You will know that you are carrying offense if you are keeping a *record of wrongs*. Playing the offense over and over in your mind,
you can't move your thoughts beyond your pain.

If you hold onto offense, this is the outcome:
condemnation, jealousy, pride, anger, unforgiveness,
bitterness, torment, depression, and a generational curse . . .
spreading to your family.

Condemnation will tear you down. It points out what a failure you are and how badly you've messed up. You will see the problem, but won't see the solution.

If you don't get in the ring, you won't get punched.
DON'T GET IN THE RING!
"Where there are many words, sin is not absent."

Ask yourself: Did I cause it? What can I learn from it?
Do I need to apologize?
Will it matter in a week, a month, or 5 years from now?
If it doesn't matter for eternity, it doesn't matter!
Calmness can lay great offenses to rest: *Keep Calm.*
Remember, humility always wins.
Wait for God's timing; He will help you take the wall down.

"Do not be easily offended."

The ·wise [insightful] ·are patient [hold in their anger];
they will be ·honored [praised; glorified] if they ignore ·insults [offenses].

> ❖ *Proverbs 19:11*
> ❖ *Expanded Bible*

Speech

Have you ever read the words "Out of Order" on a bathroom door?
That's a sign it doesn't work! There is stuff that just won't flush.
So it is with us. We often react before thinking, and spew words that
clog our lives. We end up "Out of Order."
Words have power.
The tongue has the power of DEATH and LIFE.

A tongue of DEATH is negative, complaining, perverse, gossiping,
controlling - producing shame, regret and fear.

- ❖ Our lives reflect what we say.
- ❖ Idle (negative) words cause sickness.
- ❖ *Perception and speech are linked.*
- ❖ Perverseness breaks the spirit.
- ❖ Whoever repeats a matter separates friends.
- ❖ **We get what we say.**

A tongue of **LIFE** encourages, promotes health, is peace-loving,
has a considerate nature, is sincere, merciful, impartial
and full of wisdom.

- ❖ A good word promotes life.
- ❖ Cheerful speech brings health.
- ❖ Character, love and speech are connected.
- ❖ *Perception and speech are linked.*
- ❖ Wisdom speaks the truth.
- ❖ The tongue can sing . . . Sing Life Songs!
- ❖ **We get what we say.**

*"Let the words of my mouth and the meditation of my heart be
acceptable in Your sight.".*

❖ *Psalm 19:14*

59

Value

What or who do you **value** most in life?
"Where your treasure is, so there will your heart be also."
Value is really found at the heart of the matter.
So, what's the matter?
What you worry about most, often shows what you value most.

Searching for VALUE? . . .
You matter.
You're not invisible.
Is this how you see your value? . . . "If I could just get the Who's
Who crowd to love me..." "I've got the biggest and best..."
"Wait till people see and hear me!"
We all want love and acknowledgment. The search light is on our
attempts to find approval. If we're not careful, we exasperate and
exaggerate ourselves. We end up spinning like a top with twisted
thinking, feeling plastic and devalued.

You and I have expensive alarm systems in our homes
to guard our valuables. What is really valuable is not necessarily
material, but it can still get stolen from us.
There are dark forces like spiritual pirates, invading our minds, wills,
and emotions - trying to steal our value.

When it comes down to it, real value can never be measured by the
who's who, dollars and cents, or even what we look or sound like.
**Real value can be found in how we value others and how we
value God. Love with your heart, soul, mind and strength.**

How does God value us? - To find out, value His opinion.

*His thoughts about us are more than the grains of sand on every
seashore.*

He LOVES me.

❖   *Read Psalm 139*

61

Emotions

Emotions are the product of something: bad news, good news, choices, relationships, pain, sin, and more.

God gave us our emotions and often they act like indicator lights, telling us when something is wrong.
Emotions can change from minute to minute.
We can be on a roller coaster ride, swerving with emotions.
Feelings can change; sorrow can turn to joy,
anger to rage, and love to hate.

"I FEEL . . ." (you finish the sentence)

Emotions that are out of order can put stressful demands on us. They lead to actions with great consequences if we allow our lives to be led by them.

"IF I COULD JUST . . ." (you finish the sentence)

If we end up led by emotions and not by faith,
It's DANGEROUS!

Emotions have desires and demands:
"I'LL FEEL BETTER IF I . . ." (you finish the sentence)
Out of control emotions are an enemy to your faith -
We cannot be led by God if we are led by our emotions.
Out of control emotions are a product of a heart that is not satisfied by Scripture.

We can control our emotions instead of letting our emotions control us! **Faith is not an emotion, it's a choice.**

There is a place to go to have our thinking and emotions re-wired and put back in order.

> ❖ *The address is Philippians 4:8*
> *Producing Galatians 5:22 & 23*

Regret

Regret is something that distresses you so much that you can't stop thinking about it. It upsets you right now, but only for a little while.

You and I get woken up by distress. We won't end up regretting that kind of pain if it leads to God. Think about the dead end you've been down. Did you turn around? Did you find your way out? Regret has a way out . . . it's called "hope and future."

Do you understand that when regret is full blown, you enter the place called hopelessness? You isolate and rebel against everything wise. It starts with disappointment, mostly in yourself. We've all been there a time or two. A sure sign that things are headed the wrong way is a mind that runs away - with itself, running from God. It focuses on everything negative, and carries a lot of heavy baggage.

He is the way out. He's called salvation. What you can't see is that it will all turn out right in the end. Faith believes that. Hope finds that. The song of deliverance is playing for you . . .
His Love is Unstoppable.

It gets better. You end up closer to God and closer to really living life right; awake, sensitive, responsible. Look beyond yourself, and don't look back, look forward and keep looking up. Your heart gets better, too. You find out it wasn't the hurt or who's right or wrong. You find out about freedom.

Regret always leads to the issue of the heart between us and God. We all want do-overs. Life doesn't give them, but God does. He never wants us to repeat a past performance. In fact He doesn't want performance at all. He gives us a new day, new beginnings, grace, mercy, opportunities, hope, help, courage, strength, freedom, and a brand new door when we close that old one. Yes, we have to close it. He will wait. God wants to guide our feet into the way of peace. We might think we just stumbled into it. All along, His plan was to get us there: lessons learned, no strife, quiet waters.
He leads . . . **No Regrets.**

Milestones and Markers

Within the fabric of human experience, in the human lifespan,
there are milestones and markers. Points of reference on the journey of
life. They are given on purpose, for our purpose.

Birth, death, marriage, divorce, graduation, successes, holidays,
celebrations, failures and pain. Life is full of milestones and markers.
Are you suffering because of a painful marker in your life?
If you allow for the process of the pain, you gain understanding
and you will find the treasure in the trial.

In life, milestones and markers indicate the need for a blessing.
Mark the milestones of those you love with kindness and
encouragement. Give a blessing whenever you can.
It can be the marker of healing to a hurting person.

Milestones and markers bring wisdom.
Life takes time. We learn true love in a lifetime.
Belief in living is not separate from daily life.
You live what you believe.

Today is the beginning of a new season.
A season precious and wonderful for you. A milestone of life and a
marker of Truth.
It's really up to you. Receive it and believe it!

You didn't get those gray hairs, wrinkles, and scars for nothing.

Mark the milestones of your mercy and love, God.

❖ *Read Psalm 25*

TMI

Too Much Information . . . usually *gossip*.
"Where there are many words, sin is not absent."

Troublemakers start fights. Gossips break up friendships.
Where there are drama-wars and sideshow distractions,
emotions take over and destruct like a tornado.

When we feel guilty, it's usually because we are.
Immaturity has no boundaries. Cowards go behind backs;
never face-to-face. Cowards always have a goal in mind, to ruin a
reputation. Whose company are you keeping?
Be careful. Like spirits attract.

If you run out of wood, the fire goes out. When the gossip ends,
the quarrel dies down. Life has a way of coming around.
Gossips can end up speechless.

FYI - For your information . . .
A wise person takes advice. Trustworthy people keep secrets. People
who are busy helping others, stay out of trouble. Their lives are
uncontaminated by self-interest. They are open to God, leaving no
room for counterfeit faith. They are models of goodness.
They glow in the dark.

Words have more power than we really understand.

"The Silence is the secret. In the quiet is the mystery.
Silence your body to listen to your words. Silence your tongue to
listen to your thoughts. Silence your thoughts to listen to your heart.
Silence your heart to listen to your spirit.
Silence your spirit to listen to His Spirit. Leave the many to be with
the One." ~ Mama Maggie Gobran

Desperation or Grace?

It's been written that every day one of two things happen:
"We either feed our confusion or strengthen our clarity."
(Read that again slowly.)

We often live in quiet desperation, waiting until the
"urgent need" is so pressurized it has to be addressed . . .
RIGHT NOW! We end up reckless, dangerous or in full abandonment
and risking it all. Desperate people do desperate things.

"That's not me," you might say.

Key Signs: When things come under pressure does your vocabulary
change? Do you resort to intimidation, manipulation, control or
obsession?

Fear never makes the right choice.

The Exit Sign reads: **GRACE**. It's the only way out.

God's grace is a gift and it needs to be received with humility. It's the
life preserver to rescue and save us from ourselves. Grace is God's
touch on our desperation,
"Right here, Right now."

So when you receive grace, pay it forward. Extend grace to someone
today...especially on the road.

Grace is amazing!

*"God is good to one and all; everything he does is suffused with
grace."*

❖ *Psalm 145: 9*

Present Thinking

". . . I am not happy. Nobody cares. It won't make a difference.
God doesn't hear me. They'll think I'm stupid. I have no money.
I have no time. I'll never make it. I'll never get chosen. I'm not pretty.
God doesn't speak to me. I've done all this, and look what I get for it.
I'm not loved. I'm afraid, I'm confused. I don't know.
I want to end it all."

Present Thinking . . .

Today is a gift.
God, what are you trying to tell me?

I know the plans I have for you; your times are in My Hands.
Trust Me.
Hope is in you because I put it there.
I want you to succeed.
Don't let your expectations of others cripple you.
Look to Me.
Communion dispels confusion.
I'm sending you an angel to tell you, *"Don't be afraid"*
I'm breathing life into your life.
Listen for Me. Talk to Me.
I've got your purpose on purpose.
I made you to be excellent, not perfect.
You can be excellent at everything good today.
I judge you innocent.
Make the choice to use your beautiful feet to walk away from evil.
You are loved.

Today is a gift . . . *Can you be content with that?*

The Road to Freedom

There is no such thing as part freedom. ~ Nelson Mandela

Never say never. That's a dead-end road.
Our lives are meant to be lived free. So why are so many of us so stuck?
Maybe there's a root. When bitterness breaks the surface, it consumes
who we are.
That root has to be killed.

On the road again? We may have to travel it more than once.
The road to freedom takes courage. You'll be more courageous with
your armor on. (Ephesians 6:10-18)
You will come across roadblocks every day; that's where trusting God
comes in. The road gets lonely and dark at times; that's where prayer
comes in. Sometimes it's like walking a tightrope; that's where
obedience and discipline come in.
Don't worry, God has a net underneath you.
What will you see on this narrow road? Look for a pillar-
cloud and fire - guidance and light.

Everything that happens on this road is for a reason,
You don't know, you don't know, until you know.
When truth comes alive, it makes us alive!

So what's stopping you? Fear, fret and worry. Or road rage.

"The secret to freedom is a brave heart." ~ Thucydides

Take the first step - trust. It's the hardest, but when you do,
you'll begin to feel yourself again. Take a lot of deep breaths
and keep looking up. It's the beginning of something great!

"Focus on the journey, not the destination."~ Greg Anderson

You arrive when understanding comes that your freedom has already
been paid for and you know who paid it forward for you. That root of
bitterness that you had is finally dead.
You're free.

Cost

Life struggles and troubles . . . they cost.
Relationships lost in battles. Health issues.
Money lovers now stripped.
Kids without hope, who can't cope.
Economy and job loss, promises broken.
Our world is constantly in damage assessment.

How much does it cost?
We are so aware of that question in our life of needs, desires, lusts and wants. To everything there is a cost.
But so often we don't count it, until it's too late.
Woulda, shoulda, coulda is deada.
The truth is, we all would do things differently.
So let's do things differently.

There is something that we can't buy with money.
It's very expensive, it costs our time:
Time away from TV, facebook, comfort, popularity, pleasure and sleep. It's something that looks forward, moves forward, and doesn't give up. It's something that is powerful, and alive with answers about our future. It's necessary, urgent, determined, hope-filled, and persevering. Not motivated by a food, by popularity, by who's watching, or even by a crisis, but motivated by a relationship with God.

Prayer costs. Love spilled out extravagantly.

"Answers came today, because somebody prayed."
"God moves mountains, but faith and prayer move God."

Count the cost.

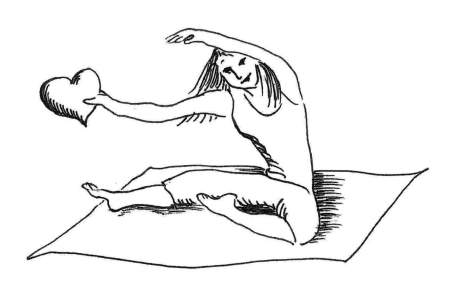

Obedience

"Love is the key. Love is the answer. Love is the greatest tool. Love is the greatest weapon. Love." ~ David Wagner

Obedience is a choice motivated by love.
Obedience is the outcome of a life formed out of miracle words- from the pages of the Greatest Book.
People who walk in obedience are people of prayer.
Obedience walks us toward our future goals . . .

"Does it make sense to pray for guidance about the future if we are not obeying the thing that lies before us today?"
~ Elisabeth Elliot

Being wise about what is good and innocent about what is evil -
that's real discernment that leads to obedience.
Obedience S_T_R_E_T_C_H_E_S our faith to go beyond
what we are capable of, into what God is able to do.
Doesn't it feel good to stretch?
Obedience can be learned through suffering.

How do we obey right here, right now?
We start by asking for a willing mind and heart.
Once your mind is there, your feet will follow.

Choose to love someone today. Obey the greatest command.

"This is love, that we walk according to His commandments. This is the commandment, that as you have heard from the beginning, you should walk in it."

❖   *2 John 1:6*

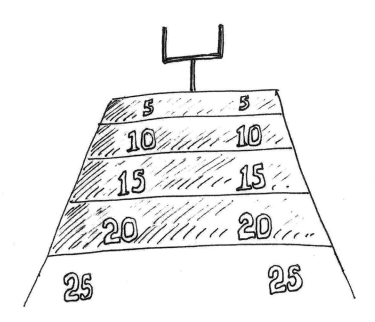

The Red Zone

Red is the color of passion, anger, blood, and love.

In football, it's the part of the field
where scoring is most likely to take place.

Are you in the **red zone** today?
If so, your character is being revealed.

What's needed?
Strategy, relationship, tenacity, faith . . .
blood, sweat and tears.

Sometimes there's only one chance.
Start with the decision to try, but not without Him.
Include GOD in the huddle and watch what happens.
He has a timing and it's perfect.

There is a power within you and me, a power that is often untapped
until we're in the **red zone.**

That power, if used properly, expects and tastes victory.
The goal is . . . love from a pure heart, a good conscience, and a sincere
faith –
love uncontaminated by self-interest and counterfeit faith.

A life open to God . . . ***Touchdown!***

Happiness

Are you in pursuit of happiness?
Are you driving around looking for it? Are you enjoying life?
Is happiness a state of mind or just a vacation?

When people live well, honest and happy, they glow with light;
the longer they live, the brighter they shine. Their faces are always
radiant. You have a lot to be glad about - more than you think.
Smile, you're breathing right now.

Remember that old saying that money brings happiness?
Well, listen to this . . . *"Money is as short-lived as a wildflower,*
so don't ever count on it. You know that as soon as the sun rises,
pouring down its scorching heat, the flower withers. Its petals wilt
and, before you know it, that beautiful face is a barren stem. Well,
that's a picture of the "money life." At the very moment everyone is
looking on in admiration, it fades away to nothing"
❖ (The Message)

Happiness: Even when it rains, God is in every drop.
Good news makes the heart glad.
A heart in the right place is tuned up, it sings, it gives,
It's happy!

He who has mercy on the poor, happy *is* he.
If you give from the heart, **Happy Happens**.
(That should be a bumper-sticker)

Celebrate those you love.
Let's face tomorrow with a bigger smile.
There is a longing God wants to fulfill and it's called
the **desire of your heart.**
One condition: find out how to be happy in God.

"Delight yourself in the Lord and He shall give you the desires of your
heart."
❖ Psalm 37:4

Kisses and Betrayal

Kisses come in many forms.
"An honest answer is like a kiss on the lips."
"Wounds from a sincere friend are better than many kisses
from an enemy."
"She began to wet his feet with her tears. Then she wiped them with
her hair, kissed them and poured perfume on them."
"The one I kiss is the man; arrest him."

The Kiss of Death . . . Betrayal.
A stranger may be able to hurt you, or deceive you,
but only someone you care about deeply can betray you.
"Even my own familiar friend in whom I trusted, who ate my bread,
has lifted up his heel against me."
Betrayed? Stabbed in the back? Didn't see that coming?

Are you playing a game with God called
The Make - BELIEVER?
Wearing two faces: one for offense and one for defense.
Haven't we all been on both sides, or off sides?
A Penalty Occurs: sorrow, set back, and pain.
The hit was so hard, that a catastrophic emotional hole opens.
Reaction: Speechless! Questioning! Heartbroken!
Salt pours through words. The point of no return - Revenge.
We WALL UP and say "NEVER."
The inner vow takes hold like a pit-bull and results in the destruction
of the soul. Kiss it goodbye.
GAME OVER.

God's Kiss - Forgiveness.
"A woman close to death was told she was so close to Jesus she should
feel for His kisses. She asked one thing;
'Pray that he never stops kissing me."

His words are kisses: His kisses, His words.

Will Power!

His will is His Word.
He doesn't want us to get over it. He wants us to go through it.

Do you want Hope? Forgiveness? Redemption?

"People are often unreasonable, irrational, and self-centered. Forgive them anyway.

If you are kind, people may accuse you of selfish, ulterior motives. Be kind anyway.

If you are successful, you will win some unfaithful friends and some genuine enemies. Succeed anyway.

If you are honest and sincere people may deceive you. Be honest and sincere anyway.

What you spend years creating, others could destroy overnight. Create anyway.

If you find serenity and happiness, some may be jealous. Be happy anyway.

The good you do today, will often be forgotten. Do good anyway.

Give the best you have, and it will never be enough. Give your best anyway. In the final analysis, it is between you and God. It was never between you and them anyway."

~ Mother Theresa

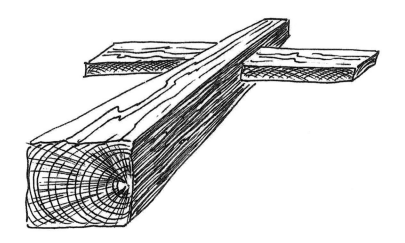

OMG

Oh My God! Haven't we all said that a few thousand times?
The element of surprise, shock, dilemma, awe -
something we don't expect.
The take-our-breath-away moments of life.

This is an amazing journey we are all a part of called life.
Did you ever read this? *"Teach us to number our days."*
Don't waste your life, **LIVE YOUR LIFE!**

No matter what "Oh My God moment" you are in, good or bad,
there is real opportunity in it to learn.
Be present in the moment.

Today, don't waste time, it's very expensive.
And don't keep doing the same thing. You know you'll get the same
results. We are all under construction on the inside, being changed
mostly by our trials. We end up *pressure-treated,* then we can take on
the storms.

To those who overcome great obstacles, life is amazing.
Be an overcomer. Faith is required.
If you've prayed for something, now relax.
Do you believe He heard you?

Every time God reveals a new part of us, or every time He strips off a
layer and reveals the next one, we have that incredible
"Ah-ha" moment - **Oh My God!** Don't take yourself so seriously, God
might not. He is not limited by anything or anyone.
Even if you don't believe in Him, *He believes in you.*

So call out **"Oh My God"** to Him, not in vain, but in honor.
He hears you every time. After all - it's His name.

Voice

How many people will you talk to in the course of a day?
Do you ever feel clouded by too many voices?
What about the voices in your own mind? Which one can you trust?

The television speaks, and most of the messages we hear from it are
false. Deception always holds a little bit of truth, that's how it deceives.

We don't have to be in the same room to recognize the voice
of those we love. We know their voice by the sound and the tone.
We can even tell how someone feels just by their voice.

Do you recognize the voice of God the same way?

Some thoughts:
   ❖ Hearing requires listening . . . *carefully*.
   ❖ If we really seek the truth, it's hard not to hear.
   ❖ God doesn't play a game with guidance. He never contradicts
     Himself.
   ❖ Face the Book . . . and read it out loud.
   ❖ You can have a private appointment with God, right now!
   ❖ Prayer has an answer.
   ❖ Creation speaks of God. Go outside.
   ❖ Is hearing His voice the highest priority of your day?

"My sheep hear my voice, and I know them, and they follow me."

   ❖ *John 10:27*

Vision

Is the sky the limit? Or, is it to infinity and beyond?

The problem with vision is, we can get so caught up in yesterday
that we can't see where we are going today.
Let go of blaming the past so you don't hinder your ability
to see to the future.

Ready or not, here it comes! A new day - no mistakes in it yet.
It's full of vision, waiting for someone to seize it.

Hide and Seek, we play that game with God -
at times hiding from Him. Our excuses keep us blindfolded,
but the key is to SEEK Him with everything we've got.

He is the Light! He wants to reveal direction, instruction, confirmation,
and vision.

*"Impossible is nothing, and nothing is impossible
because with God all things are possible."*

Vision . . . it looks up, and creates something out of nothing.
It sees the possibilities and finds solutions.

If you really want more vision, go to a place where
you become smaller and God becomes bigger.

"Where there is no vision, the people perish."

❖   *Proverbs 29:18*

Capacity

Is your cup running over? Are you half-full or half-empty?
If you're full of it, what is "it" that you're full of?
For the mouth speaks what's in the heart.

We all struggle in one way or another.
Are you at the breaking point? Let it go - whatever that "it" might be.
Look how small **"it"** is. Do you find yourself saying,
 "I can't take it anymore!?"

Yes, you can!

Take a deep breath. Open your heart. Move out of the way
and let God's plan in. Nothing in His Plan is a waste of time or effort.
It's not over until He says so. And, don't forget He's Eternal.
He has our backs and our battles. Our times are in His Hands. Ready
or not, tomorrow is coming!

We were born with resilience, so spring up!
Bounce back! Look up!
Fill your tank with the High-Test:
Perseverance, Endurance, Surrender.
That is full capacity!

We do get more than we can handle at times. Storms are inevitable and
sometimes the **"it"** is a tragedy, it's no small thing.
I heard a wise man say, *"Make the decision not to turn your back on
God, no matter what."* Then the tragedy can turn to triumph.
You will live a life full of compassion and mercy, overflowing with
thankfulness in the midst of the heartbreak.

Capacity . . . *Enlarge my heart, God.*

Crossed Your Mind?

If it's crossing your mind, maybe it's God's prompting.
Occurring suddenly, don't ignore it! Think about it.

If there is a cross in your mind, it's the intersection between obedience
and disregard. You choose which way to go.
Make the call. Knock on the door. Text the message.
Email the letter. Send the flowers. Ask for forgiveness.

What's necessary? At times, humility.

You've been asked quietly . . . don't dismiss that thought.
Listen closely.

It may mean sacrifice. It may mean humbling.
It may mean you have been wrong.

This is your opportunity, take it! Just do it!
It may mean everything . . . FREEDOM. HEALING. LOVE.

What are you waiting for? Follow the prompt.
If you have the means to help . . .
Put your sneakers on – RUN TO DO IT!

See what happens . . .

You will be part of a MIRACLE!

Traction

Sometimes we need a push –
P.U.S.H. – **P**ray **U**ntil **S**omething **H**appens.
Prayer belongs to Heaven and forces us forward.

Are you between a rock and a hard place?
Spinning your wheels? Kicking up a lot of dirt?
To make matters worse – someone sees your dirt, and judges.

How do I get out of this? How did I get into this?
No matter which way I turn, I don't see the way forward.
I feel so stuck . . . If you're constantly looking back, that will only sink
you deeper.

Traction . . .
We need traction when we're stuck.
Sometimes we have to dig out one shovelful at a time.
Facing the reality of our life and choosing not to hide from it.
Find something to get a hold of, something that grips.
Spiritual Traction . . . Healing Hope – that point of contact
in our mind when we grab hold of "perseverance."
That determination will wrap around those revolving thoughts
and grip onto Hope. Then we'll gain momentum -
No disappointment.

Now plow out . . .
Get out of "playpen prayer meetings" and "playing church."
Take the new tool you got from this experience and use it today.

Get up and look up!
Do all you can do and leave the rest up to God.
That's really where the rubber meets the road . . . *Traction.*

Signs

Do you need a SIGN? How about water?
He opens the heavens and the Rainmaker pours it out on the earth.
Not enough? Do you need a promise?
Open His book, there are thousands in it.
Do you need a key? Open your mouth.
His Word in your mouth is life.
Encouragement sparkles.

Signs are everywhere; sometimes they say STOP.
Listen well. There is a whisper in the wind.
Be open. **Today has an answer in it.**

Are you praying for a sign?
Take a walk outside alone through the parted sea before you.
Oh, it's there, can't you see it? It's that trail that was blazed in front of
you - likely, by your Mom or Dad. Or, maybe by that amazing friend
who prayed for you.

**The thing about signs; they're confirmed by miracles and
wonders.**

*"In the Last Days," God says, "I will pour out my Spirit
on every kind of people: Your sons will prophesy, also your
daughters; your young men will see visions, your old men dream
dreams. When the time comes, I'll pour out my Spirit
On those who serve me, men and women both, and they'll prophesy.
I'll set wonders in the sky above and signs on the earth below, Blood
and fire and billowing smoke, the sun turning black and the moon
blood-red, Before the Day of the Lord arrives, the Day tremendous
and marvelous;
And whoever calls out for help to me, God, will be saved."*

❖ *Acts 2:19 The Message*

Medicine or Poison

Recently, Diane Sawyer reported on *World News Tonight* that more people are dying from prescription drug-related deaths than in car accidents.

Attitude and health are connected. Often, our attitude may need adjustment. That would take an adjustment in our speech.
The same mouth can kiss and spit. These days, people can tame wild tigers, but we just can't tame our tongues. The poison from our own words may defeat us, if we are not careful with them.

"Where there are many words, sin is not absent."
Poison comes in the form of gossip, and separates good old friends. Poison winks, points, lies, and destroys tranquility in the heart of man or woman. The next thing we know, we need medication because of a confused mind.
We drink it down . . . *just like poison.*

There is a prescription from God that brings life and health to us. It just takes some studying:

"The tongue of the wise person promotes health."
"People with merry hearts do good like medicine."
"A good report makes the bones healthy."
"A good word makes the heart glad."
"A faithful ambassador brings health."
"An honest answer is like a kiss on the lips."
"A gentle answer turns away anger."
**"Pleasant words are like a honeycomb - sweet to the
  soul, and health to the body."**

Medicine or Poison?

"A wholesome tongue is a tree of life."
                                ❖   *Proverbs 15:4*

Stretch & Strength

We get stretched to get strengthened - *Stretching us to believe.*
Spiritually, faith can mean strength . . .
"If you fail under pressure, your strength is too small."

We get stretched by transitions.
Desperation and pressure stretch us.
We all need a larger capacity to resist fear.
What saps your strength? You already know that answer.
Don't do it all on your own strength.
Power under control - that's real strength (meekness).
The secret to strength is surrender.
"Don't be wise in your own eyes."
You will need stronger glasses . . . Wisdom beyond your own.

Gather your strength: encouragement, honor, obedience, good news, quietness, confidence and rest.
When the soul prospers, there is wholeness mind, body, and spirit.

"I can do all things through Christ who gives me strength."
"He renews my strength."
"He is my refuge and strength."
"God strengthens the hearts of people who are fully committed to him."

Clothe yourself in strength. Put the armor on.

"Love the Lord with your heart, soul, mind, and strength."

"I will love you, O Lord, my strength."

❖ *Psalm 18:1*

Peace

"A people free to choose will always choose peace."
                                    ~ Ronald Reagan

Peace remains silent.

"It's not the absence of conflict, but the ability to cope with it."

Give the gift of a peace offering and receive one back.
Peace can be multiplied.
Love, truth, and peace kiss . . . kiss that way.

Enter every house and speak peace in it. Watch what happens.
Send people away in peace when they leave you, you never know when you will see them again.
Give an answer of peace and watch everything change.
Peace like a river; flows out gently.
A smile brings peace.

God holds our peace as He fights for us.
Righteousness and peace go together.

"When a man's ways please the Lord, He makes even his enemies be at peace with him."
                              ❖ *Proverbs 16:7*

The Prince of Peace has perfect peace.
Those who know His words, have His Peace.

Read the Gospel of Peace.

Victory

Without a battle, there cannot be a victory.
There is a cost and a cause - if it's important enough, we run toward
the bullets.

The emotional, physical or spiritual battle we fight, takes a
single-eyed made-up mind. A mind, determined and trained –
one that won't be denied. Fight the good fight of faith –
Armor On!

The battle on our knees is the most important. Often, the real battle is
to get into that position. When you do, rehearse the victories
and learn from the defeats.

The war is really over the big three: Fear. Worry. Disappointment.
If they have a track record in you, break those records -
especially the ones you play over and over in your mind.

*"My brothers and sisters [fellow believers], when you have many
kinds of ·troubles [trials; testing], ·you should be full of joy [consider
it all/pure joy], because you know that these troubles test your faith,
and this will give you ·patience [perserverance; endurance]."*

❖ *James 1:2-3*
Expanded Bible

Celebrate Victory! Raise the flag. Take the trophy. Wear the crown.
Stay ready, another battle awaits another victory.

*"For God so loved the World that He gave only begotten Son, that
whoever believes in Him shall not perish but have everlasting life."*

❖ *John 3:16*

Understanding Easter, That's Victory!

Rest

Rest . . . or restless?
The road to resting: How are you going to get there?
Not by running away from it all.

Rest is a PROMISE. Rest is HOLY.
God wants to give you the Rest . . . of your life.
The question becomes: Forced Rest or Willing Rest?

We are in a world full of pain and anxiety.
What causes unrest? - Pain in any area.
Marks of unrest: exasperation, turmoil, confusion, striving,
sleeplessness, anger, fear, frenzy, depression, unnecessary guilt,
shame, fretting, worry and regret.

The "rest reserves" get used up.
Sleep deprived? #1 reason we age fast.
When you experience overwhelming doom, it multiplies . . .
If you worry, so will your kids! Statistics tell us, the number of children
suffering from anxiety is off the charts.

"Will all your worries add a single moment to your life?"
❖ *Matthew 6:27*

"Don't give in to worry or anger; it only leads to trouble."
❖ *Psalm 37:8*

Real rest needs quiet and it starts in your mind.
**In order for your mind to rest, your tongue has to rest.
Stop talking about it!**

Real rest has peace as a partner and surpasses your understanding.
Marks of Rest: security, trust, provision, hope, joy, and an even
temper, and love. Rest allows you to sing and dance.
God is at Rest Right Now!

*"Come to Me, all you who labor and are heavy laden, and I will give
you rest."*
❖ *Matthew 11:28*

Author of Life

He makes Himself known.

He is The Creator, The Source, The Originator, The Designer,
The Inventor, The Expert, The One and Only – God.
He is behind the scenes - responsible for your existence and mine.

He writes life; man writes eulogies.
He writes sacred things - things that cause motion, inspiration and
circulation. He reveals eternal things that matter, from His heart to
ours. He is waiting, and wanting us to welcome His Words . . .
Freedom Words.

It is written: *"It takes more than bread to really live"*. . .
It takes every Word from God's mouth. Every Word Counts!
Get ready, roll up your sleeves, shift your mind into gear,
totally ready to receive. He is so personal and up close, you could feel
His breath and His heartbeat. He breathes understanding into a man.
Inhale.

There is life that comes from His flawless Word.
Don't forget. Collect the words. Write them on the tablet of your heart.
This adds time and years. Life becomes satisfying.
Read on . . . *Proverbs 3*. And when you're done, **Exhale.**
Echo over and over what He said. Say it loud, Say it clear,
and Say it forward with confidence and authority.

The truth from the Author of Life is in you and me.

Goodbye Song

"Go find your dream.
Go take a chance.
Go make it count, live and dance.

Give yourself fully to your desires.
Your heart trusts, you're ready to inspire.

Hope is waiting and love will survive.
When you step in fully, everything will come alive.

Keep your eyes looking up and your heart in faith.
He will guide your steps, for His goodness sake.

Every time you say you're goodbye,
Be sure it's completed or go back and try.
Then you will dance to the goodbye song -
With no regrets as you move along.

Love is big, it opens doors -
All hoping and praying, watching you soar.

The goodbye song isn't sad.
Where you're going, will make hearts glad.

So dance in your prayers with great expectation.
For God in His love, has given you salvation."

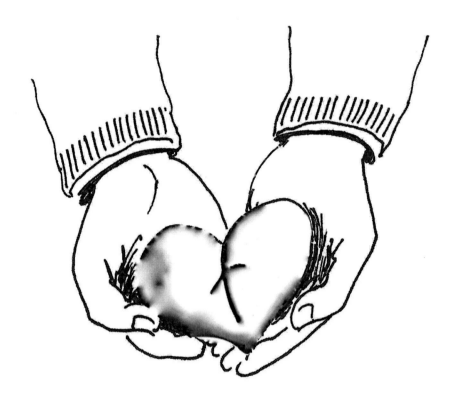

Final Prayer

A prayer can never be answered until it is prayed.
Please take a moment, and pray this with me:

God,

*I open my heart and pray to You, The One and only One
who holds every answer to every question. My prayer to You today is
to ask You to renew my prayer life, so that it flies - not with a broken
wing, but with freedom, ease, perseverance and purpose. With the
kind of prayer that connects me to your heart, so when I pray, I
would feel your presence all around me.*

*Thank you for letting me know that my prayer links me to your will
and your will is your Word.*

*In your Word, it was asked, "Teach us to pray."
You answered:*

*"But when you pray, go away by yourself, all alone, and shut the door
behind you and pray to your Father secretly, and your Father, who
knows your secrets, will reward you."*

*"And when I stand praying, if I hold anything against anyone,
I forgive them, so that You, my Father in Heaven,
may forgive me my sins."*

*I believe that I will receive whatever I ask for in prayer -
in your way and in your time because I know You love me.*

And . . . I love you.

Notes & References

1. (LIFE)
   "That's Life" song written by Kelly L. Gordon, Dean Kay; Bibo Music Publishing, Inc., 1966

2. (NEW BEGINNINGS)
   Zechariah 4:10 - *The Message* by Eugene Peterson; Navpress, 1906, 1999

3. (HOPE)
   Romans 5:3-5 - *The Expanded Bible*; Thomas Nelson, 2011

4. (FOCUS)
   Luke 16:13 - *New Living Translation*, Tyndale House Publishers, 1996, 2004, 2007
   Matthew 6:22 -*The Voice Bible*; Ecclesia Bible Society, Harper Collins, 2013
   2 Chronicles 16:9 - *The Amplified Bible*; The Lockman Foundation, 1987

5. (THE GREAT WALL OF OFFENSE)
   Proverbs 19:11 - *The Expanded Bible* (Ibid)

6. (REGRET)
   "Unstoppable" (Rascal Flats song) written by James Slater, Jay Demarcus, Hillary Lindsey; Chrysalis One Music Publishing Group Ireland, SONY/ATV Tree Publishing, 2009

7. (DESPERATION OR GRACE?)
   "We either feed our confusion or strengthen our clarity"
   Behavior Never Lies; Richard Flint
   Psalm 145 – *The Message (Ibid)*

8. (FINAL PRAYER)
   Matthew 6:6 – The Living Bible; Tyndale House, 2013

9. Except where noted, all Scripture quotations are taken from the New King James Version, copyright 1982 by Thomas Nelson, Inc. All rights reserved.

CPSIA information can be obtained at www.ICGtesting.com
Printed in the USA
BVOW04s0552110414

350364BV00006B/36/P